THE
KIRK OF THE
GREYFRIARS
EDINBURGH

by
PROFESSOR ALAN STEELE

—

with illustrations by
SIR ANTHONY WHEELER

—

The Society of Friends of the
Kirk of the Greyfriars
MCMXCIII

First published 1993 by
The Society of Friends of the Kirk of the Greyfriars
Copyright © All rights reserved
The support of Lothian and Edinburgh Enterprise Limited in the
production of this guidebook is gratefully acknowledged
Designed and typeset in Caslon by Dalrymple
Printed in Scotland by Alna Press
ISBN 0 9521115 0 0

Preface

✥

THE CONGREGATION AND THE FRIENDS OF GREYFRIARS are indebted to Professor Alan Steele for his concise but thorough resumé of Greyfriars' complex story; also to Sir Anthony Wheeler for agreeing to provide the splendid artwork.

Those of us who worship regularly in this building love it very much. The many changes to the fabric and furnishings since it was first dedicated make us more than ever conscious of the continuity of worship that has taken place here. Generation after generation of Edinburgh's citizens, academics, tourists, school children and students have experienced here something of the holiness of God and been warmed by the love of God.

We hope that all who visit Greyfriars now will also go out feeling they have been in touch with the eternal and the good; and that this guide will evoke happy recollections of their visit.

Prayers are offered regularly by the congregation for our visitors. We appreciate your prayers for us, and for the church's ongoing work and witness.

DAVID BECKETT
Minister

The Mausoleums of the Adam and Robertson families in the Churchyard

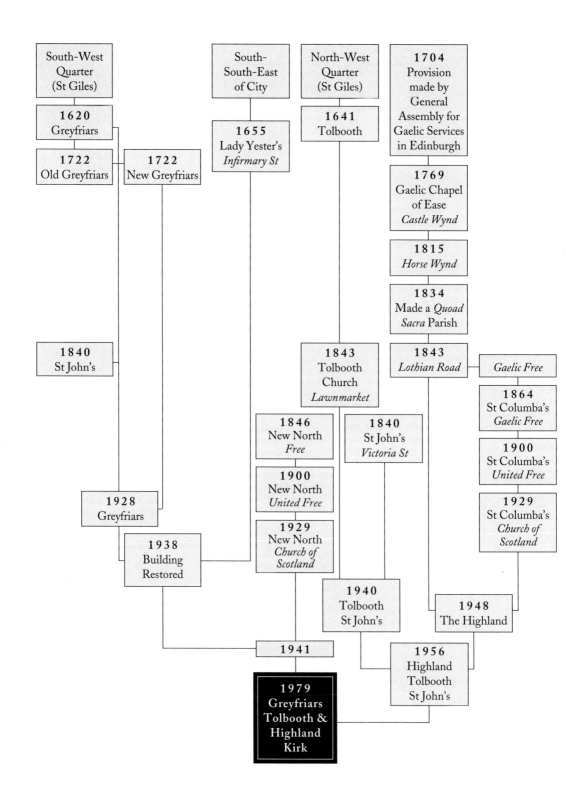

South-West Quarter (St Giles)

1620 Greyfriars

1722 Old Greyfriars

1722 New Greyfriars

1840 St John's

1928 Greyfriars

South-South-East of City

1655 Lady Yester's *Infirmary St*

1938 Building Restored

North-West Quarter (St Giles)

1641 Tolbooth

1843 Tolbooth Church *Lawnmarket*

1846 New North *Free*

1900 New North *United Free*

1929 New North *Church of Scotland*

1840 St John's *Victoria St*

1704 Provision made by General Assembly for Gaelic Services in Edinburgh

1769 Gaelic Chapel of Ease *Castle Wynd*

1815 *Horse Wynd*

1834 Made a *Quoad Sacra* Parish

1843 *Lothian Road*

Gaelic Free

1864 St Columba's *Gaelic Free*

1900 St Columba's *United Free*

1929 St Columba's *Church of Scotland*

1940 Tolbooth St John's

1948 The Highland

1941

1956 Highland Tolbooth St John's

1979 Greyfriars Tolbooth & Highland Kirk

The Building & its Dramatic History

⁓✦⁓

THE KIRK OF THE GREYFRIARS, famous in the annals of Edinburgh and the history of the Scottish Church, stands in the midst of its quiet, green kirkyard, shielded from the noise and stir of the city. Outwardly, it is very plain for so large a church, having neither tower nor transept nor clerestory, and very little decoration; the interior, however, is spacious and airy, furnished with unpretentious dignity, and enlivened by the colours of its windows.

Greyfriars was the first church built in Edinburgh after the Reformation. It takes its name from the Franciscan friary that had stood at the eastern end of the Grassmarket from the time of James I until 1558. In 1562 the town council was allowed by Mary Queen of Scots to take over the grounds of the former friary for use as a burial yard, the space around St Giles being already more than filled and a danger to public health. By the end of the sixteenth century the High Kirk itself (as St Giles is properly called) could no longer accommodate the growing population of the town, and in 1601 the council decided that it would have to move out the 'south-west quarter' – one of the four parishes which at that time shared the High Kirk (subdivided for the purpose). It was agreed that the most convenient site was 'the buriall yard quhair sumtyme was situat the Grey Frieris', and stonework from the derelict nunnery of St Catherine of Siena (in what we still call the Sciennes district) was to be brought to the site and re-used. Progress was slow, however: only in 1611 did the council get so far as to decide that 'the kirk foundit in the buriall yaird suld be biggit with pilleris'. A date-stone from 1614, bearing the burgh arms, can be seen high up on the eastern gable, but the Kirk was not opened for regular use until Christmas day of 1620.

The external appearance of the Kirk as it then was is preserved in Gordon of Rothiemay's view of Edinburgh, published in 1647. It was an aisled building of six bays, with buttresses, a squat square tower at the west end, doorways on the north, south, and east, and a timid touch of fantasy at the east gable. The interior was no less austere – a bare rectangle, devoid (as one would expect) of chancel, chapels, statuary, or coloured glass. There were, however, the 'pilleris' – five octagonal piers on either side, linked by pointed arcades marking off the aisles from the nave. At the time in question, such features were a Gothic hang-over, and it has been suggested that this anachronism might have been a reminiscence of the parent High Kirk; perhaps, though, it was merely the simplest way of holding up the wide roof. In any case, the pillars certainly add interest to the interior. There were lofts on the east and west sides, probably also on the north. Some 'paynting and cullouring' was carried out, though precisely of what is not known. Furnishings would be very few – limited perhaps to the pulpit set against the mid south pier, and from 1636 a stool of repentance. For communion services, trestle tables and benches would be brought in – a practice which remained normal in Scotland until the later nineteenth century.

Such as they were, the furnishings had to be renewed, and no doubt much else had to be made good, after the Kirk had been used as a cavalry barracks by Cromwell's troops from 1650 to 1653. As John Nicoll wrote in his diary (July 1656), 'the College Kirk, the Grey Frier Kirk, and that Kirk callit Lady Yesteris Kirk, the Hie Schule, and the great part of the college of Edinburgh wer all wasted, their pulpites, deskes, loftes, saittes, windois, dures, lockes, bandis, and all uther their decormentis were all dung doun by these Inglische sodgires, and brint to asses'.

In 1684 the magistrates, dissatisfied with the appearance of the tower, considered topping it with an ornamental spire. It was just as well, however, that

The entrance to Greyfriars from Forrest Road

this plan was not carried out, for in the early hours of Sunday 7th May 1718, the tower, used by the town council for the safe storage of gunpowder away from the city centre, blew up, laying the west end of the Kirk in ruins. The four eastmost bays, still useable, were hastily closed off by a wall, and it was decided to build a new kirk, symmetrical with the surviving eastern part and in the same 'plain Gothick', abutting on the outer face of the new wall. The cost was met from a local duty on ale. Alexander McGill was appointed architect, and the work was completed in 1722. Thus there were now two churches under the same roof – Old Greyfriars and New (or Wester) Greyfriars, each with its own parish and its own ministry. (An earlier division of the original building, intended to increase the number of parishes in Edinburgh, had lasted only from 1656 to 1662). At the new west end a low, small porch was built, and as the new west gable had a pediment, one was added also to the east gable (though with straight skews over the aisles, not wavy Dutch-style skews as at the west end). The buttresses, old and new, were topped with the pinnacles and balls they still carry today. The reconstruction was completed by the building of a portico in the Palladian manner on the north side, giving access to both churches, and with two vestries on its upper floor reached by a wooden turnpike stair. Inside New Greyfriars, there were lofts on the north, south, and west; the pulpit, as in the original building, was set against the mid south pier, and the piers were painted to resemble veined marble.

Some 120 years later, on 19th January 1845, a disastrous fire caused by the overheating of a boiler flue gutted Old Greyfriars, seriously damaging also the roof and much of the furniture of New Greyfriars. Coming so soon after the Disruption of 1843, this catastrophe was regarded by some as a divine judgement on the established Church. Hugh Miller the famous geologist, writing in the Free Church periodical *The Witness*, expressed the wish that the buildings should not be restored: there was room for both congregations in St John's church in Victoria Street, while with the addition of some ivy judiciously planted round the walls Greyfriars would make an interesting ruin... In fact, however, New Greyfriars was at once put to rights, the north, south, and east lofts rebuilt with Gothic panelling in front, and a high canopied pulpit set now against the west gable. Old Greyfriars. though, presented a much more serious problem. There, during the preliminary work, part of the north arcade collapsed, killing one workman and injuring two others. So the city architect,

David Cousin, decided to remove the remaining arcades, and to span the building with a vast open timber roof. In addition to this major surgery, the windows were given simple lancet tracery in the Early English style and, at the wish of the minister, Dr Robert Lee, glazed with coloured glass – probably the first in any Scottish parish church since the Reformation. Now without arcades or lofts, Old Greyfriars was re-opened in 1857.

Thereafter, save for some details, the two Kirks remained virtually unchanged until 1932. In that year, however, following the reunion of the two congregations in 1928, and supported by a national appeal for funds, work was begun to restore the arcades, the roof, and the gable of Old Greyfriars; and in 1938, after some 220 years, the dividing wall was removed, so that there was once more a single Kirk. However, the two westmost bays still remain distinct from the rest: though the nave runs right through to the west gable, the aisles have here been formed into rooms, with a gallery across the gable. To this extent, the identity of the original six-bay building has been restored, and is further emphasized by the great roof-high arch. Henry F. Kerr was the architect responsible for this reconstruction.

In 1989 a gallery was built across the nave under the great arch, to carry the new organ. (The story of organs and music in Greyfriars is dealt with separately, p.15). A new stair, given in memory of Sir Peter Macdonald, and made from some of the pitch-pine pews now replaced by chairs, leads up to the organ gallery from the north aisle. The architect for these works was Tom Gray. To the west of the great arch a Visitor Centre is being developed, together with improved catering and other service facilities. These and other related works, including the organ itself, have been financed through an Appeal launched in 1987 by the Society of Friends of the Kirk of the Greyfriars, and administered by a committee under the chairmanship of the Hon. Lord Davidson.

Originally the building had no bell, and in 1641 it was arranged that the bell of the Magdalene Chapel in the Cowgate should be rung to summon worshippers to Greyfriars; in 1684 an old bell from the Tron Kirk was hung in the Greyfriars tower, and replaced by a new one in 1690. After the destruction of the tower in 1718, however, the building remained bell-less until 1991, when the bell now to be seen on the north side of the porch was presented by Mrs Nancy Bryson in memory of her husband. It was cast about 1860-70, in steel, not bronze, and hung originally in St Paul's church, Waterhouses, County Durham.

Greyfriars in Scottish Life

~∂⊱~

MUCH OF WHAT HAS HAPPENED in Greyfriars has been of more than merely parochial significance in the history of Church and nation.

Following the Reformation there was a period of confusion during which the episcopalian structure inherited from the past, and favoured by James VI, co-existed uncomfortably with the new presbyterian structure of sessions, presbyteries, synods, and General Assembly. The first recorded use made of Greyfriars, in fact, before its official opening, was for the funeral service of William Couper, Bishop of Galloway, in 1619; and if Christmas day was chosen for the opening in 1620, this was because the officiating minister, Patrick Galloway, wanted 'to say something for holy days, and to please the King'. Charles I, however, tried to go much further than his cannier father, and, as is well known, his attempt to introduce a new Prayer Book in 1637 led to a riot in St Giles. There was trouble in other churches also: it is reported that James Fairlie, minister at Greyfriars, had to flee from the building, 'pursued by a mob of cursing women, "he also cursing them"' (David Stevenson, *The Covenanters*, 1988).

On 28th February of the following year there took place the most momentous event in the history of Greyfriars – the public adoption of the National Covenant (as we now call it). It was read out from the pulpit, and then signed by the nobles and gentry present – in the church itself and not, as legend has it, in the kirkyard. The next day it was signed by ministers and burgh representatives in the Tailors' Hall in the Cowgate, and on days following by the citizenry in other churches. Copies were sent to many other parts of the country for signature, and one of these can be seen in Greyfriars; what is believed to be the original is now displayed in the City Museum (Huntly House, in the Canongate). The background and implications of this event, political and economic as well as religious, are far more complex than is often supposed, and indeed the question of episcopacy is not explicitly raised in the Covenant; its main thrust, however, is unmistakeable – the Scottish Church is not a tool of the State. Whilst reaffirming their loyalty to the Crown, the signatories denied it any right to interfere in the doctrine, worship, or polity of the Church.

This is not the place to retrace in detail the turbulent history of the half-century following – the Bishops' Wars, the Solemn League and Covenant of

(9)

St John's Aisle, with the Ker memorial

1643 with the English Parliamentarians, the breakdown of this alliance because of divided opinions and loyalties on both sides, the attempts of the 'Engagers' to assist the monarchy by force of arms in exchange for the promise of a presbyterian establishment, the consequent invasion of Scotland by Cromwell, his crushing victory at Dunbar (1650), the decade of Cromwellian administration... Cromwell himself is said to have preached in Greyfriars kirkyard; he certainly used the Kirk as a cavalry barracks (see p.6). It is said also that General Monck announced in Greyfriars his intention to march on London in support of the Restoration.

The re-establishment of episcopacy at the Restoration was actively resisted by many in Scotland. Robert Traill, minister of Greyfriars from 1649, was forced into exile in Holland. Following the victory of Monmouth over the Covenanters at Bothwell Brig in 1679, more than a thousand prisoners were held for months in an open field adjoining the present kirkyard, pending trial or recantation. But the Cameronian 'Remnant' went on meeting in their conventicles throughout the 'killing time' of the 1680s, and their last martyr, James Renwick, is commemorated with his predecessors on the Martyrs' Monument. Several relics of the Covenanting times can be seen in the Kirk.

The 'Revolution Settlement' of 1690, through which the Church of Scotland in its presbyterian form was at last 'by law established', brought to an end both the pretensions of the Crown over the Church in matters spiritual, and the theocratic ambitions of the Covenant extremists. It even went some little way in the direction of toleration, since it did not declare that presbyterianism alone conformed to the Scriptures. King William explicitly enjoined moderation on the Church. His chief adviser in Scotland, largely responsible for the Settlement, was William Carstares, who became minister of Greyfriars in 1703 (before his translation to the High Kirk in 1707) and at the same time Principal of the University of Edinburgh.

The most distinguished of Carstares's successors in both these offices, William Robertson, was inducted to Old Greyfriars in 1761, and became Principal the following year. Coincidence from time to time of the offices of minister and of Principal (or, in several cases, of professor) is only one of the many links between the Kirk and the great University that lies within its parish. Indeed, in the absence of a chapel at all comparable with those of the three other ancient Scottish universities, Greyfriars has long fulfilled some of the functions of a 'university church', though having no official status as such.

William Robertson became the leader of the 'Moderates' in the Church of his day. Renowned throughout Europe and America as a historian, and the first Historiographer Royal for Scotland since the Union, he was an outstanding figure in the Scottish Enlightenment. He enjoyed the friendship and respect of the great philosopher David Hume (the 'Great Infidel', as he was called) – who also received understanding and support from Robert Wallace, minister of New Greyfriars from 1733 to 1738. (It is probable that Hume would come to Greyfriars on occasion – though it would scarcely be to worship...)

Robertson's 'Moderates' were a party of liberal and latitudinarian tendency. Opposed to them were the more pietistic 'Evangelicals', who remained closer to the Puritan or Covenanting tradition; they resented in particular the Act of Patronage of 1712 which, as they rightly thought, encroached on the independence of the Church that had been promised in the Revolution Settlement. (This question of patronage distressed the Church throughout the eighteenth century, and led indeed to the great Disruption of 1843) By coincidence, John Erskine, a leader of the Evangelicals, held the second charge in Old Greyfriars alongside Robertson... The two appear, however, to have remained on friendly terms. Walter Scott, who attended Greyfriars in his youth, gives an impression of Erskine's preaching in his novel *Guy Mannering*.

Greyfriars has always been closely in touch not only with the University, but with the whole community around it. Thus, the children of three famous Edinburgh 'hospitals' – George Heriot's, the Merchant Maidens, and George Watson's – all attended Sunday worship in the Greyfriars Kirks, from the time of their respective foundations until, in the later nineteenth century, these institutions were converted into schools of the modern type. The link with Heriot's is the oldest, going back to the dedication service on 27th June 1659, and to this day the school uses the Kirk for its end-of-term services.

The two Greyfriars churches shared conspicuously too in the philanthropic home-mission work characteristic of the nineteenth century. In 1840 the second charge in Old Greyfriars was detached to a new extension church – St John's in Victoria Street – and with it was translated the incumbent, Thomas Guthrie, who became famous as a pioneer in social work among the young and founded the first 'Ragged School', in Ramsay Lane. His statue stands in Princes Street Gardens. Then, in 1843, following the Disruption, William

Robertson (no relation of his namesake already mentioned) was appointed to New Greyfriars, and carried out invaluable work in the slums of the Grassmarket, among those whom a later writer describes as 'starved and heathenized children, growing up to be the criminals of their generation'. To-day, through its Kirk House in Candlemaker Row, the congregation maintains its interest in the now very different, yet still often under-privileged life of the people on its doorstep.

If the Disruption had thus been the occasion of a pioneering ministry in New Greyfriars, the same is true in a quite different way of Old Greyfriars, where the incumbent had also left to join the seceded Free Church, taking most of his congregation with him. In his place came Robert Lee, who in 1847 was also appointed as the University's first Professor of Biblical Criticism. Lee used the opportunity of the 1845 conflagration (see p.7) to have coloured glass windows put into his rebuilt church, and also an organ. Moreover, through a Service Book of his own devising (1857), he sought to move the Church of Scotland away from aridity in worship and undue reliance on immediate inspiration in prayers and preaching. Though in part a restoration of practices introduced by John Knox, but done away with in the 1645 Directory of Worship (largely inspired by English Puritanism), Lee's liturgical reforms – what has been called 'the Greyfriars rebellion' – were highly controversial at the time, and only a sudden illness halted the action brought against him at the 1868 General Assembly. In the event, however, his influence was far-reaching, both in Scotland and beyond. He was one of the founders, too, of the Church Service Society, whose library is still kept in the Kirk.

In 1938 the two congregations were brought together again under one roof (see p.8). They were joined in the same year by the former Lady Yester's congregation, and in 1941 by the congregation from New North. These were both churches of historical significance: Lady Yester's had in former times been the University's official place of worship, and the New North church (United Free) was in the early years of the twentieth century a main centre of attraction for Edinburgh students. Finally, in 1979, came the union with the congregation from the Tolbooth church on Castle Hill, itself originally, like Greyfriars, an off-shoot of the High Kirk (1641), and with which St John's and the Highland Church had already been united. Thus was formed the congregation that now worships here under the name of Greyfriars Tolbooth and Highland Kirk. Part of the agreement was that services in Gaelic should be maintained – and in fact Greyfriars is now the only parish church in south-east Scotland where such services, distinctive in their mode of worship as well as in their language, are regularly held, in addition of course to the services in English. In this way, yet another strand, one of peculiar interest and value, has been woven into the rich tapestry of the Greyfriars heritage.

Given this heritage, it is not surprising that Greyfriars today should seek to maintain an open-minded and welcoming attitude, a readiness to experiment, and to engage with the many activities that go on in the city around it, remembering always that the Kirk is nothing if it is not a place for prayer, meditation, praise, spiritual refreshment, and creative work done in God's name.

The south side, after the restoration of 1938

Organs & Music in Greyfriars

Ever since Dr Lee brought an organ into the Kirk (see p.13), thereby breaking through a centuries-old inhibition in the Church of Scotland, good music – choral, solo, and instrumental – has been cultivated in Greyfriars.

Dr Lee started with a harmonium, but this was soon replaced by a pipe organ, which stood against the wall dividing Old from New Greyfriars. In 1889, New Greyfriars in its turn installed an organ against its own side of the wall. This instrument had been built originally, in 1866, for the Park Church in Glasgow by the Edinburgh firm of Hamilton, and was at the time the largest organ in Scotland. When the two Kirks were reunited in 1938, the Hamilton

The organ by Peter Collins at the west end of the nave

organ was retained, and the other, no longer needed, was sold to St Columba's Church, Blackhall, where (after renovation) it is still in use; the Hamilton organ, after undergoing some brutal surgery, was very inappropriately relocated in the north-west loft, thus being masked by the arcade, while the console was placed at floor level under the arcade on the opposite side of the church, with the choir nearby. Nor were things at all improved musically when, in the 1950s, both choir and console were removed to the east end of the building, some forty yards or so away from the instrument. So, in 1988, when the organ had to be replaced, it was decided to set the new instrument, together with console and choir, on a gallery built across the nave for this purpose – an arrangement leaving room at floor level for an orchestra or an augmented choir when required.

The new organ, built by Peter Collins, has three manuals (Great, Swell, Positive), and a pedal department in separate flanking towers, with the 32' pipes concealed beneath the back gallery floor. The action is mechanical, but the 50 stops are electrically actuated. A few of the more unusual registers of the Hamilton organ have been retained. A brochure is available giving detailed information about this important instrument.

Greyfriars also posseses a chamber organ, built by Hamilton in the 1840s, and purchased from its previous owners in 1970. It has eight stops on two manuals.

The Greyfriars Choral Society, founded in 1865 by Joseph Geoghegan, Robert Lee's musical adviser, for many years led the worship, performed concerts and recitals, and was regarded as the leading choir in the city. Its high standards have been fully maintained by the present-day choir, and this tradition can now, with greatly improved facilities, be further strengthened.

Since 1979, music in Greyfriars has been further enriched by the Gaelic services, where the Psalms are sung unaccompanied, and with the characteristic Celtic ornamentation.

A Look Around the Interior

When one enters the Kirk from the north porch, past the iron-studded oak doors, the general impression is one of well-proportioned spaciousness. The plain plaster-rendered walls of nave and aisles set off to advantage the simple pattern of the piers and arcades, the varied colours of the windows, the ceiling of Californian redwood, the medium oak of the panelling, pulpit, organ-case, gallery and stairs, besides the blue of the chancel carpet and the seating. The ornamentation is everywhere restrained, and the whole composition has an un-ostentatious elegance, with the occasional touch of bravura in the windows or the organ.

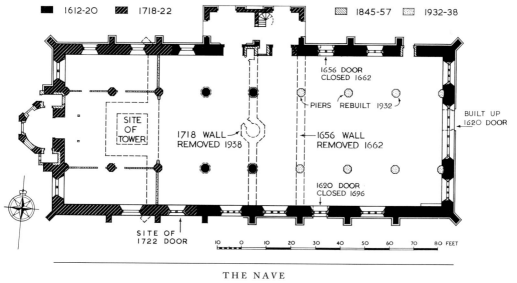

THE NAVE

The orientation of the building may be due to the lie of the land rather than to ecclesiastical tradition, but along with the Gothic-style architecture it suggests the east end as a major focus of attention, and this is certainly the case. The oak panelling there dates from 1912, though modified by George Hay in 1971 – as too was the communion table of the same date; in their original form both were the work of Herbert Honeyman, who also created the raised area on which the table stands. The bronze plaques on the table front show a Gospel author at work, and the traditional symbols of the four evangelists. Forming part of the stone floor is a small pavement of green and white marble from Iona and purple marble from Skyros in the isles of Greece.

The Franciscan symbol of the Five Wounds of Christ figures discreetly in the central canopy of the reredos. The gilt cross and crown were presented in 1963 by 432 City of Edinburgh Corps Engineer Regiment (Territorial Army), which had long been based in the parish. On the south side of the raised area is a marble font, brought from Rome in 1912 by W. Moir Bryce (author of *The Scottish Greyfriars*), along with the pedestal, possibly dating from the early Renaissance period. The blue carpet, part of the one laid in the nave of Westminster Abbey for the Queen's coronation in 1953, was presented by the Friends of the Kirk of the Greyfriars.

The east end of the nave

Prominently set against the third south pier stands the pulpit. Built in 1912 by Honeyman in seventeenth-century style, it was modified in 1951 by George Hay and moved here from its earlier location at the north-west corner of the raised area around the communion table, so that it now occupies the same position as did the pulpit in the church of 1620. An inscription at its base com-memorates the signing here of the National Covenant in 1638 (see p.9). The shields under the tester are those of Scotland, the city of Edinburgh, and Edin-burgh University. Round the edge of the tester runs the Latin text of St John's Gospel I, 14: 'And the Word was made flesh and dwelt among us, full of grace and truth'.

The pulpit

In the panelled ceiling of the nave, dating from the 1930s, are five medallions bearing the emblems of the Father, the Son, and the Holy Ghost, of St Andrew, and of St Margaret, Queen of Scotland from 1069 to 1093.

Westward, under the great arch where it originally terminated, the nave is dominated by the impressive new organ, with its soaring towers, its trumpets *en chamade*, its delicate carvings by Derek Riley showing Scottish fauna and flora in panels derived from seven-teenth-century French designs, besides the head of a Franciscan friar, and the famous Skye terrier 'Greyfriars Bobby'. Along the frieze of the towers runs the inscription *Laudet Dominum omne quod spirat* – the Latin form of the last verse of the Psalter, 'Let every thing that hath breath praise the Lord'.

Around the space behind the organ are painted plaques showing a variety of Christian symbols, some of Pictish derivation, presented in 1936 in memory of the wife of Dr W. W. D. Gardiner (see p.22) and of his mother.

THE NORTH AISLE

The communion table at the east end came from the New North church. On the north wall, Robert Lee (see p.13) is commemorated by a marble head and nearby by the angel of the Resurrection, both sculptured in high relief by John Hutchison (1870). In the corner, the Stars and Stripes, presented by the American Consul General in 1970, recalls that 350 years earlier the landing of the Pilgrim Fathers in the New World and the opening of Greyfriars took place on the same day.

Further west, a plaque commemorates Robert Wallace, successor to his friend Robert Lee in 1868, and who later became editor of *The Scotsman* newspaper. At the west end, above the organ gallery stair, is an 'Act of Parliament clock', brought here from the Tolbooth church. (Such clocks were so called because of the tax imposed upon them in 1797 by William Pitt.)

THE SOUTH AISLE

Since the union with Lady Yester's in 1938, the eastern part has been known as Lady Yester's Aisle. On the south wall is a fine memorial tablet, brought from that other church, and nearby is the stone that marked Lady Yester's grave. The lectern, carved from a single block of oak, also came from Lady Yester's Church. The communion table is from New Greyfriars.

The western part, now known as St John's Aisle, has been used since 1979 for the Gaelic services (see p.14); the furnishings here came from the St John's (Gaelic) Chapel in the Tolbooth Church. The west wall carries a touching family memorial; on the south wall a tablet commemorates the philologist Thomas Ruddiman, David Hume's predecessor as Keeper of the Advocates' Library, and responsible for the first collected edition of the works of George Buchanan (1715).

Between these two named Aisles, on the south wall, a handsome stone tablet commemorates Scotland's greatest architect, Robert Adam (1728-1792). It follows one of his own designs, and was erected in 1992 to mark the bicentenary of his death. (The Adam family mausoleum is in the kirkyard, but he himself is buried in Westminster Abbey).

A little further to the east is a brass tablet to the memory of Alexander Nisbet, one of the leading authorities on Scottish heraldry, incorporating his own arms as Chief of the Name of Nisbet. Further east again, an oak panel recalls that in his youth Walter Scott worshipped in Greyfriars – but does not add that he subsequently became an Episcopalian.

THE WINDOWS

The coloured windows in the eastern part of the building date from the 1850s and are of special historical interest (see p.8). With the exception of the tartan-like Anderson window in the north aisle, the work of Francis Barnett, they are all by the firm of Ballantine and Allen, and are basically grisaille, with abstract patterning. The central five-light window in the east gable, however, has four medallions illustrating the parables of the Prodigal Son, the Wise and Foolish Virgins, the Good Samaritan, and the Pharisee and the Publican in the Temple. Flanking it on the north is a window in memory of John Erskine and one on the south honouring William Robertson, with a medallion representing St Luke as Historian. (See p.12 on these two ministers). The first window in the south aisle, showing St Paul preaching to the Athenians, is in honour of John Inglis, minister in Old Greyfriars from 1799 to 1834 and remembered for his promotion of missionary work in India. The one next to it commemorates the Covenanting minister Robert Traill (see p.11).

From the same period, by James Ballantine, is the spectacular heraldic window celebrating the great Renaissance man of letters George Buchanan, tutor to James VI, who died in 1582, and is buried in the kirkyard. The central panel shows at the foot the arms of Buchanan of that Ilk, and at the top the crest of Buchanan of Drumikill, George's great-grandfather. The quotation beneath the portrait, from an epitaph by the contemporary French philologist Joseph Scaliger, alludes to his pre-eminence as a neo-Latin poet: 'Once the limit of the Roman empire, Scotland will mark henceforth the furthest reach of Roman eloquence'. The side panels are each topped by the royal crest, surmounting on the left the royal arms, and on the right the national badge of Scotland – the St Andrew's Cross or Saltire. Each of these bears the motto *Nemo me impune lacessit* (commonly rendered in Scots as 'Wha daur meddle wi' me?'), of which Buchanan is sometimes said, but is not certainly known, to have been the

Looking towards Lady Yester's Aisle,
with the Robertson window

author. At the base of the right panel is the Star of the Order of the Thistle, with the same motto, though the badge certainly, and probably the Order itself, did not exist in Buchanan's day. On the other side is a seal used informally by Mary Queen of Scots, with a coat of arms reflecting her claim to the thrones of Scotland, France, England, and Ireland. Buchanan had been welcome at Mary's court, but after the murder of Darnley he became one of her fiercest enemies. The open book higher up displays a fragment from one of his works, together with a facsimile of his signature, while the Scots harp opposite, with a thistle wreath and a palm branch, symbolizes his status and fame as a poet. (A leaflet giving a fuller account of this window is available in the Kirk)

The St John Baptist window further west was brought here from the Tolbooth Church after the union of 1979. It had been presented by the well-known artist, Sir D. Y. Cameron (d.1945). A very cool and elegant composition, it commemorates the witness of St John's Church in Victoria Street (see p.12). The next window, by Marjorie Kemp, is warmer in tone, though still hieratic. It is a tribute to Helen Pearl Gardiner (d.1936), wife of Dr W.W.D. Gardiner, during whose ministry and thanks largely to whose initiative the reuniting of the two Greyfriars churches took place. The Latin quotation is from the twelfth-century hymn *Jesus, thou joy of loving hearts* ... and reads 'But what to those who find?'.

The central west window, by Ballantine and Gardiner, dates from 1898. Much more romantic in manner, it represents the morning of the Resurrection.

THE VISITOR CENTRE

This is currently being developed at the west end of the kirk. Among the objects on display is one of the original copies of the National Covenant (see p.9), besides a number of relics of the Covenanting times, portraits of leading figures in the movement, and replicas of banners carried at the battle of Bothwell Brig.

A series of engravings shows the exterior and interior of the building at various stages of its history. Also to be seen is a replica of the 'cutty stool' or stool of penitence (see p.6) which is now kept in the Royal Museum of Scotland in Queen's Street. The fine seventeenth-century silver communion and baptismal vessels owned by Greyfriars are displayed in the same Museum.

Of interest to many visitors is the portrait of 'Greyfriars Bobby' painted from life by J. McLeod in 1867.

Included in the Visitor Centre is a sales point operated by the Society of Friends of Greyfriars.

John Hutchison's marble head of Robert Lee
on the north wall

(23)

Eternal God,
in love you have sustained the worship
and the witness of this place
throughout the years.

Be with those who serve here now.

Renew in me the sense of your abiding presence.

Bless my coming in
and my going out, and help me
in my daily living
to fulfil your hope and trust;
through Jesus Christ
our Lord.